MG
SPORTS CARS

John Heilig

MBI Publishing
Company

To Florence, for her love and understanding, especially during the MG years; and to Susan, Sharon, Laura, and their men, who make it all worthwhile.

First published in 1996 by MBI Publishing Company, PO Box 1, 729 Prospect Avenue, Osceola, WI 54020-0001 USA

© John A. Heilig, 1996

MBI Publishing Company books are also available at discounts in bulk quantity for industrial or sales-promotional use. For details write to Special Sales Manager at Motorbooks International Wholesalers & Distributors, 729 Prospect Avenue, PO Box 1, Osceola, WI 54020-0001 USA.

Library of Congress Cataloging-in-Publication Data

Heilig, John.
  MG sports cars/John A. Heilig.
    p. cm.—(MBI Publishing Company enthusiast color series)
  Includes index.
  ISBN 0-7603-0112-3 (pbk. : alk. paper)
  1. M.G. automobile—History. I. Title. II. Series: Enthusiast color series.
TL215.M2H45   1996
629.222—dc20   95-26552

On the front cover: This immaculate 1948 MG TC is owned by Pete and Fran Thelander; on the right, Chip Pedersen's equally stunning 1957 MGA Roadster. *Dave Gooley*

On the frontispiece: Grille detail of Sis and Bob Eschelman's 1955 MGTF.

On the title pages: Bernie Rapaport's 1966 MG Midget MkII. *Dave Gooley*

On the back cover: The mid-engined MGF, introduced in 1995 by the Rover Group. *Rover*

Printed in China

Contents

Introduction

I feel confident in saying I wouldn't be the person I am today if it wasn't for MGs. Two in particular.

When I got out of the Army in 1960, I drove my parents' 1951 Ford for a couple of months. But I was single, making a decent salary, and had friends who were into sports cars. When the opportunity arose for me to buy an MGA, I grabbed it. I can't even remember how much I paid for the car, but I'm certain it was under $1,000, more like $800.

That MG introduced me to a whole new universe of people. I discovered rallying, racing, gymkhanas, and a lot about myself and cars. I became an "enthusiast." I joined the Newburgh (NY) Sports Car Organization (NESCO), whose mascot was the Road Runner from Warner Brothers cartoons. I met a few young women, one of whom owned an MGA coupe, another of whom was eventually to become my wife.

When I changed jobs the MGA came with me. One day, on the way home from work, the master cylinder blew and I had no brakes. Using the hand brake I was able to maneuver to the local MG dealer, who told me it would cost about $80 to repair the master cylinder. I couldn't afford that kind of money, but I could use the roadster as a trade-in on the coupe he had in the showroom. I now had my second MG and a much happier girlfriend-soon-to-be-wife, who appreciated the better weather protection afforded by the coupe.

When I wanted a reduced-rate subscription to *Safety Fast*, the MG Car Club magazine, I started an MG Car Club in New Jersey. I met more great friends.

When my new employer suggested I take a technical writing course, I complied. But the teacher taught *writing*, not just technical writing, and he turned me on to something I never liked in school. He said, "Write about what you like." I liked cars. I wrote about my MG. Stuart Seager and Wilson McComb, who were running *Safety Fast* in those days, encouraged me by buying my first article, which compared American rallying to

European rallying. They also bought my second, a report on the (Long Island) MG Car Club International 1000 Rally. I was hooked.

When I parlayed these two stories into a weekly motorsports column for my local paper, I knew I had found a new profession. Unfortunately, it took more than twenty-five years to get out of the old one and into the one I wanted all along. When Bell Laboratories suggested I take advantage of an early retirement package, I jumped ship and began working for a newspaper. Two years later, I joined the staff of *Automobile Quarterly*.

If I hadn't bought the first MG, I probably wouldn't have become a motorhead, wouldn't have had the nerve to drive down to where I met the woman who would eventually become my wife, wouldn't have started writing, and wouldn't be the person I am today. But I did and am and I thank you for buying this book. I hope I have transmitted some of the love I held for these cars.

As with all projects, this couldn't have been completed without the help of a lot of friends—some old and some new. In fact, in the course of meeting new friends, we got back in touch with some old ones. My rally driver, Dave Holt, and his wife Marilyn and my wife and I had lost touch when we moved out of state. However, so many people with whom I spoke were friends of Dave's, who is still an MG owner, that I had to call. So thanks first to Dave and Marilyn for the good MG years of the 1960s, along with Lee and Carolyn Wescott, and Bob and Jean Ross—both of whom are unfortunately no longer with us.

For this project, I thank all the owners who made their cars available for photography: Rob Van Sickle, George Iacocca, Mike Jones, Sis and Bob Eschleman, Wade Cruse, Terry Kozo, Lance Babbitt, Joyce Tucker, Pete Ernst, Bob Hulshouser, Art King, and Jonathan Stein. Thanks, too, to Dave Gooley and Mike Mueller for their photographic assistance.

This book wouldn't be in its final form without the persnickety editing assistance of my office-mate, Karla Rosenbusch. She's so good with a comma. And its final form is the work of the ever interesting Jane Mausser and Zack Miller of Motorbooks, who continue to have faith in me.

A rare Tickford-bodied MG TA at a "Gathering of
the Faithful" meet in California. *Dave Gooley*

① Before the War

In the beginning there was William Morris. No, not the talent agent, the car builder. Morris founded Morris Motors early in the twentieth century, hired some forward-looking people who saw more in his Morris cars than mere utilitarian transportation, and lived to see the sports car that arose from the minds of these people eventually outlast the cars that provided the components.

Today, the name MG is far better known throughout the world than Morris, and even though the car's life was in a state of suspended animation for several years, it is showing a resurgence in the late 1990s that may allow it to celebrate its 100th anniversary in 2023.

William Morris was born in 1877 in Cowley, Oxford, England. When William was young, his father became ill and the youngster had to step in and become the family breadwinner. At the tender age of sixteen, he set up a bicycle repair shop behind his family's house. Even though the prime purpose of the business was bicycle repair, Morris soon branched out into building custom bicycles.

In 1901, Morris moved into larger quarters to build his cycles. Two years later he added small engines to the bicycles and began building motorcycles. Before long, he made the logical next step and began selling and repairing automobiles. In 1910, he moved again, to a new location in Oxford. The facility was first known as The Morris Garage and was renamed The Morris Garages in 1913.

Morris assembled his first car from purchased parts in 1912. In 1913, the first Morris Oxford was offered for sale at £175 ($875).

This was all very normal for the early movers and shakers in the automobile industry on both sides of the Atlantic. Morris continued to build his little cars after a short hiatus during World War I when he manufactured munitions to support the British war effort. Morris Motors, Ltd. was formed in 1919, but The Morris Garages was kept separate.

Cecil Kimber joined The Morris Garages, Ltd. in 1921 after serving stints with A.C. Cars and the E.G. Wrigley Company, a supplier of axles and steering gears to automobile manufacturers. Kimber demonstrated his business acumen in a paper on factory organization that was published in 1916 and in an earlier treatise in which he went into the details of the costs of operating his Singer 10. Kimber was originally hired as sales manager for The Morris Garages. One year later, the general manager of the company committed suicide. Kimber was asked to take his place.

Meanwhile, Morris Motors continued to build cars. In 1914, the first Morris Chummy appeared. This was a two-seater body on a Morris chassis. Kimber saw this model and decided to build his own version. In 1922, the first Morris Garages Chummy was built, with an 11.9hp Cowley engine. This car was the spiritual ancestor of the MG sports cars.

According to Phil Jennings, writing in *Automobile Quarterly,* "It was not until late 1923 that the cars built by The Morris Garages were given the MG name." Kimber said later that he was looking for something more distinctive than the basic Morris car when he built the Chummy. Jennings said that although the car "did not wear an MG badge, it most surely signaled the birth of the marque."

Kimber's Chummy had a two-seater body that left little room for a third passenger. Later two-seaters had room for a third

MG founder Cecil Kimber in FC7900, his Morris Special, known as Old Number One. While Kimber used this car to win the 1925 Land's End Trial, it prob-ably wasn't the first MG. In fact, Kimber sold the car and it was finally bought back by the company several years later. *Collection of the author*

passenger over the rear axle. The Morris Garages Chummy was lower than the Morris version because the quarter elliptical springs used in the rear were mounted above the chassis frame rather than below it. Carbodies of Coventry built the bodies. Kimber added leather upholstery to offer something extra.

The first Chummy was sold in August 1923 for £300 ($1,500).

Interestingly, the car revered as "Old Number One" by MG owners over the years, Kimber's Special with plate number FC7900, was not the first MG. It was most definitely one of the first, but it wasn't *the* first. Instead, FC7900 was a 14/28 with a special one-off body that Kimber used to win a gold medal in the 1925 Lands End Trial. The 14/28 desig-

nation connoted a taxable 14hp with an actual 28hp from the 1802cc four cylinder engine. The production version of Kimber's Special, the "Super Sports," which was produced from late 1924 to late 1926, had a windshield and sold in England for $1,680.

The first car to wear the distinctive MG octagon badge was a 1926 14/28, based on a Morris Bullnose. This car had a flat angular radiator with a 3in-tall skeletonized nickel silver "MG" attached to the radiator matrix. Jennings added, "the round Bullnose 14/28 radiator badge was still there but the central shields were gone, having been replaced by a small MG octagon badge."

So, by the end of the 1920s, all the elements were in place, except one. MG was

The M-Type is recognized as being the first true MG Midget—the first of a long line of sports cars. *Collection of the author*

building cars under its own name, having finally broken out from under the thumb of Morris Motors. But these cars were generally large sedans and convertibles that can be compared more with a modern Chrysler LeBaron convertible than with a Mazda Miata.

One variation of this trend was the MG 18/100 MkIII, developed from the MG Six Sports Mk III road-racing model. This Mark III was a racer through and through. It was priced at £895 ($4,475) and only five were built. Known as the Tiger or Tigress, it was entered in the 1930 "Double Twelve" at Brooklands, where it retired after fifty laps and 2½ hours.

In 1929, the MG Car Company, which would become the M.G. Car Company, Ltd. on July 21, 1930, introduced the M-Type Midget, England's first practical, inexpensive small sports car. The M-Type was the car that pushed MG into a new arena, an arena in which it would be a leader for many years.

The M-Type Midget was powered by an 847cc four-cylinder engine rated at some 20hp. Body weight of the little car was just 1,100lb, which guaranteed a top speed of well over 60mph. The M-Type was cheap to run and suitable for an amateur to use for competition. One of these amateurs, F. M. Montgomery, drove in the 1930 Monte Carlo Rally and broke the 1100cc class record in the Mont des Mules hillclimb with his M-Type.

MG had a new car in the wings. A 1930 prototype, EX120, used an M-Type Midget's engine destroked to 745cc and added a supercharger. This engine was installed in a chassis with a streamlined fabric body. It became the first 750cc car to go over 100 mph on February 16, 1931, when George E. T. Eyston took four records with a top speed of 103.13 mph at Montlhery.

EX120 spawned the C-Type Montlhery Midget, with a supercharged 750cc engine rated at 60hp. This was an out-and-out racing

Capt. George E.T. Eyston at the wheel of the record-breaking MG EX.120 speedster in 1930. In this car, Eyston exceeded 100mph at Montlhery in February 1931, becoming the first 750cc car to reach that speed. Eyston honored the author in 1962 when he visited the brand-new MG Car Club, North Jersey Center and spoke on MGs and Castrol Oil, a company of which he was then director. It was a fascinating visit. *Collection of the author*

The huge 18/100 Mark III "Tigress" was one of two cars prepared for the 1930 Double Twelve at Brooklands. The other was an M-Type Midget. *Collection of the author*

car that could embarrass the bigger, more powerful Bentleys of the day. The C-Type was most un-MG-like, with a front cowling that gave it a more streamlined shape, and a boat tail. Only forty-four C-Types were built.

Late in 1930 the M.G. Car Company adopted a new sales slogan, "Safety Fast," that would stand it in good stead for the rest of its life. According to MG historian F. Wilson McComb (who was also the first editor to purchase an article by this book's author in 1966), in *M.G. by McComb,* "in two words [the slogan] seemed to embody the essence of the marque's appeal." About the same time, a group of enthusiastic owners had formed the MG Car Club. Their first honorary secretary, a young accountancy student, John Thornley, joined the company in 1931; he was to be appointed its general manager twenty-one years later.

Note: There's some confusion about the name of the company and the car. Some authorities refer to M.G. before World War II, MG after. Wilson McComb calls it M.G. We refer to the company and the car as MG, except where the periods are necessary, as in the reference to the M.G. Car Company's formation in 1929.

J Series

MG continued its trip through the alphabet with the D-Type Midget and F-Type Magna, which were built from late 1931 to late 1932. These were followed by the J-series of Midgets, which were built through 1934. The J.1 and J.2 used an 847cc four, while the J.3 and J.4 used a 746cc four. Almost 2,500 of the former were built, compared to just thirty-one of the latter, with only nine J.4s produced.

An MG J.2 was the first MG to compete in an American road race when Barron Collier, Jr., drove in the Targa Florio, spon-sored by the OARC and ARCA on September 15, 1934. Briggs Cunningham also raced a J.2 in ARCA events before he stopped racing (for a while) to concentrate on the safer sport of yacht racing, at the request of his mother.

Next in MG's production line were the K-Type Magnettes—KA, KB, and K.3. The thirty-three K.3 Magnettes, including the EX135 prototype, were powered by 1087cc six-cylinder engines. The K.3s established an enviable competition record for MG, with wins in many major events. For example, George Eyston and Count Gianni Lurani won the 1100cc class in the 1933 Mille Miglia in a K.3, while Tazio Nuvolari broke the class record seven times and won the 1933 Ulster Tourist Trophy Race. His winning speed was not broken for eighteen years, until Stirling Moss drove a C-Type Jaguar to a new record.

In 1935, Sam Collier and George Rand took Collier's K3 Magnette and Rand's J.2 to Europe. According to Joel Finn's *American Road Racing: The 1930s,* "their itinerary included visiting LeMans as nondriving guests of

Displaying a very un-MG-like grille, the C-Type of the early 1930s was a potent competitor in unsuper-charged (shown) and supercharged form. *Collection of the author*

MG for the 24-hour race on June 15-16, then crossing to England and heading on to Belfast, Ireland, for the County Down Trophy race on June 22. Through the good offices of MG Sales Manager Edward Colegrove, Sam had secured an entry with the K3 for the Round the Houses race at Belfast. Sam and George then intended to spend the rest of the summer taking turns driving the MG at various continental events."

While at LeMans, the pair encountered the team of PA-type racers under the aegis of George Eyston with a team of women drivers. Entered as the Dancing Daughters, they finished as a team in twenty-fourth, twenty-fifth and twenty-sixth place. Later, one of these PAs would race at Alexandria Bay, New York, in another ARCA race.

Between 1933 and mid-1936, MG produced 6,804 vehicles in ten different model lines. Among the more attractive designs was the Airline Coupe, which was available on N-Type and P-Type chassis. The mid-1930s fastback design proved popular. The bodies were built for MG by H.W. Allingham of London.

TA

In the middle of 1936, MG introduced the TA Midget. Here was a car and model line that was to finally give MG the international

First shown in 1932, the J.2 Midget displayed the classic MG profile that would carry through until 1950. The J.2 used an 847cc four, rated at 36hp.

With 2,083 sold, it was the largest-selling MG sports car until the TA Midget of 1936-39. *Collection of the author*

Built from 1935-36, the PB Airline Coupe exhibited a fastback styling that is attractive into the 1990s. *Collection of the author*

Capt. George E.T. Eyston at the wheel of the "Magic Midget" record setter. In this car, Eyston traveled 128.63mph at Montlhery in 1933. The engine was a 746cc four previously used in "Hammy" Hamilton's J.4 Ulster Tourist Trophy car. *Collection of the author*

sales reputation it deserved to go along with its international competition reputation.

The TA followed conventional MG design practice and resembled the N-Type. The chassis as well was traditional for MG, except that the engine and gearbox were boxed in. With a 94in wheelbase and 45in track, it was larger than the conventional Midget, but had a roomy two-seat body with luggage space and a decent fuel tank.

Under the hood was a 1292cc four-cylinder pushrod four-cylinder engine that developed 52.4 hp.

Purists didn't like the new TA, which was considerably larger than previous MG Midgets. It may have been more comfortable, but when did the British ever think logically about car design? It was quieter, too, so much so that the exhaust system had to be modified to make more noise.

An Airline Coupe version was offered, but few were sold. It was replaced by a Tickford drophead coupe, which was more popular. A total of 3,003 TAs were built.

TB

The T-series continued with the TB, which was introduced in September 1939. Really nothing more than a TA with a different engine, the TB had an unfortunately short life before World War II broke out. Although engine capacity actually went down from 1292 to 1250cc, its British taxation class went up because it had a larger bore. Horsepower was increased by 2 to 54.4hp. Total TB production was only 379 before manufacturing was halted by the onset of World War II.

⯃2⯃

Postwar Rejuvenation: TC, TD, & TF

After the conclusion of World War II, returning American G.I.s brought back more than war brides. They brought back Volkswagen Beetles and they brought back MG TCs. The TC was as much a performance sports car as the Beetle was an economy car, but it, like the Beetle, started a revolution in the United States. The Beetle's revolution was toward well-built economy cars that led, eventually, to a later Japanese invasion that may have caused more harm than any war damages Japan inflicted.

The TC began the sports car revolution (or at least it's credited with being the spark that began it). And while it wasn't until several years later that the action started getting hot and heavy, the first salvos were fired by the TC.

With its vertical grille, 19in "motorcycle" tires, wire wheels, and fold-down windshield, the MG TC was the epitome of the 1940s sports car. Owner: Rob Van Syckle

As *Motor Trend*'s Jim Wright put it in 1962: "American G.I.s who were stationed in England and on the Continent, and therefore away from wives, sweethearts, mothers, Detroit advertising and other sedentary offenses, found out a car could be something more than a means of getting from here to there or something that looked good just sitting in the driveway.

"They discovered what the English and the Europeans had known all along—real driving is an art form and, besides that, it's also a lot of fun. When it came time to return Stateside many of the boys didn't want to leave these new-found thrills behind, so they looked around for something they could afford to bring back with them. Not being the millionaires our foreign cousins imagined them to be, most of them found the answer to their needs in a small, inexpensive, open two-seater than had been introduced shortly after VE Day by a small English firm in Abingdon-on-Thames. This, of course, was the now-classic MG TC, the car that is generally credited with kindling the fires of the sports car movement in this country."

The TC was really just a slightly modernized version of the TA and TB. Even though the TC was little more than a prewar TB widened slightly in the cockpit area, it was a great success. MG was able to get back into production quickly after the war by building the slightly modified TB in the factory in Abingdon, which wasn't damaged in the war.

For a car that was designed as a right-hand-drive vehicle only, the TC's dash, adapted from that of the TB, was remarkably international. A large tachometer was located

The TC had a vertical exposed fuel tank at the rear with no bumpers or overriders. Owner: Rob Van Syckle

18

in front of the driver, while the passenger had to watch the speedometer climb. He or she had a small handle to grab in case of nervousness. Fortunately, top speed of the TC was only around 75mph. Most of the other switches and controls were in the center, along with the fuel level and water temperature gauges. The instrument panel's surface was walnut veneer over plywood.

The engine was connected to a four-speed gearbox with the shifter on the floor between the seats. The shift pattern was the normal H-shape, with reverse down and to the right of fourth. The gearbox, in turn, was connected to a final drive with a 5.125:1 ratio.

Suspensions on all three models were semi-elliptic leaf springs in front and rear. This would be unacceptable in a modern car, but the solid front and rear axles still gave exhilarating handling, especially with the small engines of the day.

Under the square hood of the TC was the same 1250cc engine that had powered the TB. It was introduced in April 1939. It had a bore

The TC certainly wasn't aerodynamic, as this side view shows. Driving the TC was an exhilarating experience, especially with the windshield folded down and the wind blowing in your face. Drivers and passengers were lucky the top speed was only about 75mph.

and stroke of 66.5 x 90mm, with a compression ratio of 7.25:1. The engine used two 1-1/4in SU semi-downdraft carburetors. The cylinders fed separate exhaust ports into a four-branch manifold.

The TC was 139.5in long, 56in wide, 53in high, and weighed 1,735lb. It could go from 0-60mph in 22.7 seconds and reach the quarter mile in about the same time.

The TC's body followed standard prewar practice with an ash frame reinforced by steel and using plywood paneling. Over this, steel panels gave the car its final shape. All the lines were simple curves and basic straight shapes. There is a small bulge at the bottom of the hood at the front of the left side to clear the generator.

According to Graham Robson, "The TC was a great success, and exactly 10,000 were sold in just over four years. The TC's charm was not that it was better, faster, or cheaper than any of its competitors, but that it was there. While other companies cast around to settle on a postwar design . . . MG merely made larger and larger numbers of an old-fashioned but very appealing model.

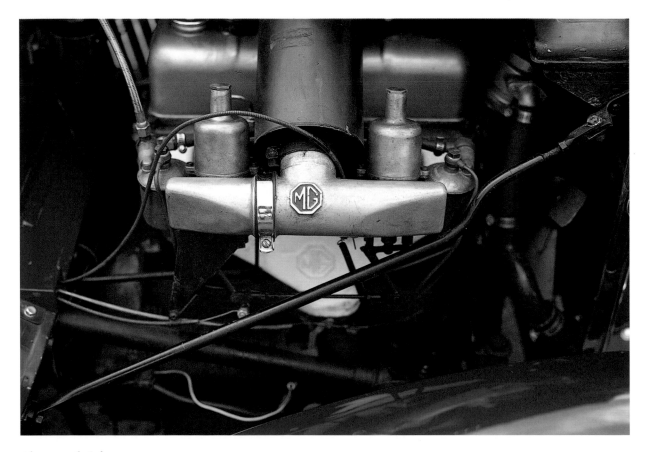

Above and right
The TC was powered by a 1250cc four-cylinder pushrod overhead valve engine rated at 54.4hp.

Carburetion was by two semi-downdraft SU carburetors.

"The TC may not have had flashy styling, but it looked rakish and was quite unmistakable for any other car. It might have had a hard ride, and old-fashioned suspension, but this gave it foolproof handling and great driver appeal."

Robson also points out that only about 2,000 of the 10,000 TCs produced were exported to the United States. However, it was the car that began the flow of sports cars that eventually included the Jaguar XK120, Triumph TR2, Austin-Healey 100, and various Singer, HRG, Riley, and Sunbeam models. When it ceased production in 1949, it had changed the world of automobiles in the United States for a long time.

MG TD

If MG had followed the trends of the other car companies after the war, the TD is the model it probably would have introduced. But it built the warmed-over TC instead, made a lot of money with it, and didn't begin TD production until 1949.

The TD was a modernized version of the prewar car, with a slightly more aerodynamic body, smaller diameter fatter tires, and a more compliant ride. With the TD came an inde-

pendent front suspension using coil springs and wishbones. The live rear axle was still located by semi-elliptic leaf springs.

Even though the TD was almost 200lb heavier than the TC, it could reach a maximum speed of 80mph. Its 0-60 time, though, was slower, at 23.5 seconds. The TD was 145in long overall, 58.6in wide, and 53in high.

While the TC had wire "motorcycle-style" wheels, the TD came equipped with disc wheels as standard equipment.

The TD used the same XPAG engine that the TC used, connected to a four-speed manual gearbox, as in the TC. Both cars also used the same rear-end ratio: 5.125:1.

One of the major changes from TC to TD was that the Lockheed drum brakes used twin leading shoes at the front. Another major change was in the front suspension. The TD used an independent front suspension that was designed by a young Morris Motors engineer named Alec Issigonis. The

With a wooden dash and the tachometer in front of the driver, any passenger was bound to be impressed by the apparent luxury, and scared to death by the speedometer needle creeping ever higher. All the critical switches were located in the center section. Owner: Rob Van Syckle

coil-and-wishbone design would be used on all MGs through the MGB. Issigonis, of course, would go on to even greater fame as the designer of the Morris (and Austin) Mini.

With its smoother lines, the TD became MG's best-selling model for its era, with over 29,000 built. Of this number, more than 20,000 were exported to the United States. In

While the similarity to the TC is evident, the TD is also a softer car. It has decent lines with the top up, a claim that could never be made for the TC. Owner: George Iacocca

fact, 28,007 of the total of 29,664 built were exported, with the next best markets being West Germany (1,248), Canada (1,146), and Australia (904). The TD ceased production in 1953 to make way for the MG TF.

MG TF

Even MG admits that the TF was "a stop-gap; an elementary 'face-lift' of the preceding model." As the London Motor Show of 1953 was nearing, MG realized that the TD wasn't

The front view shows the more enveloping fenders, wider tires, front bumper, and smaller grille of the TD as compared with the TC. The TD also had a track that was 2in wider in front and 5in wider in the rear.

going to attract a great deal of attention. After all, it had been in production for four years, and while its prewar engine had been tweaked to deliver slightly more power than in the original, it wasn't going to cut the mustard.

Furthermore, the prototype of the car that would become the MGA had been shown, and even though the project had been shelved, the handwriting was on the wall relative to the TD's lifetime.

So rather than come up with a totally new car, MG decided to smooth the lines of the TD into the TF. It wasn't a minor facelifting, either, but a major redesign of the classic TD shape. MG considered following the alphabet and calling the new car the TE, but legend has it that TE sounded too much like "tee hee," and MG didn't want people laughing every time they talked about the car. So MG skipped a letter and named the car the TF.

TF styling is what set it apart from the TC and TD. The cowl was lowered and the radiator sloped back and lowered which gave the hood line a definite angle. In addition, the front and rear fenders were reshaped and the headlights were faired in. As an added concession to modernity, the windshield wiper motor was removed from the windshield, where it had been with the TC and TD, and placed under the hood.

The driver and passenger faced a redesigned dash that was better suited to both right- and left-hand-drive models. All the instruments were set in the center of the dash in octagon-shaped bezels, while cubbyhole storage areas faced the driver and passenger. The passenger still had a grab handle for panic situations.

The exposed fuel tank in the rear was more sharply angled than before, and wire wheels were again standard equipment, replacing the discs of the TD.

Under the hood, the TF retained the same powerplant as the TD, the 1250cc unit now developing 57hp. But after July 1954, the TF was available with the new XPEG engine,

From above, the TD's smaller (than the TC) steering wheel and instrument panel changes are obvious. There's also a bit more protection for the exposed fuel tank in the rear. The TD used disc wheels rather than the wire wheels of the TC. This is a 1950 MG TD, but owner George Iacocca kept the vanity plate from the '53 TD he previously owned.

25

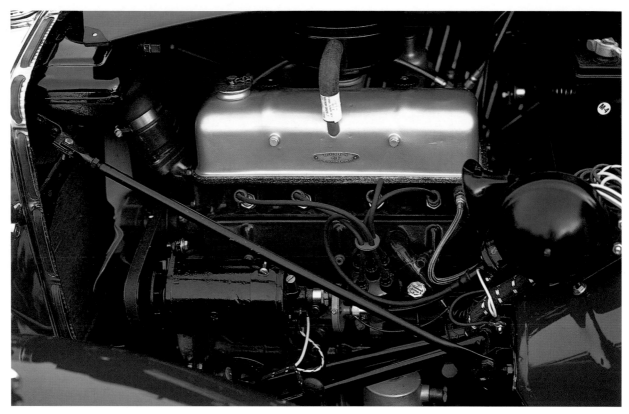

The TD used the same 1250cc engine as the TC,
rated at 54.4hp.

George Iacocca's 1950 MG TD

which was bored out to 72mm to give a total capacity of 1466cc and 63hp.

Dimensionally, the TF was 2in longer than the TD, 1in wider, and 1/2in lower. Its curb weight was about the same as the TD's.

According to *Road & Track*, the 1250 TF could go from 0-60 mph in 18.9 seconds; 16.3 seconds with the 1500cc engine. Top speed for the 1250 TF was 80 mph; 85 with the 1500. So there was a significant performance

This is perhaps one of the most attractive angles from which to view the MG TD. Owner: Mike Jones

This 1953 MG TD was George Iacocca's first car and the one for which he bought the "53 TD." It is now owned by Mike Jones.

Even with its top up, the MG TD is an attractive car with nice proportions. Some of the harshness of the more angular TC has been removed and the car seems more friendly. The smaller diameter, wider section tires help.

This view of the MG TF clearly shows the sloped fuel tank, as well as the more graceful flow to the front and rear fenders. Owners: Sis and Bob Eschelman

advantage with the TF, but it wasn't enough for the enthusiasts.

The TF didn't receive warm praise from the press of the time. Tom McCahill of *Mechanix Illustrated* called it "Mrs. Casey's dead cat, slightly warmed over." As Graham Robson said in *Collectible Automobile*, "It wasn't that the TF was a bad car. It was actually a good car, well-built and thoughtfully equipped by the standards of the thirties—but not the fifties. Not even the return of wire wheels, and all those wonderful octagonal touches, could save it."

The TF remained in production from October 1953 to February 1955, when it was replaced by the MGA.

From this angle, the cozy seating of the MG TF is evident, as is the long handbrake handle.

29

It is in the grille area where the TF displays its uniqueness. The grille is lower and smaller, while the headlights are fared into the fenders. Owners: Sis and Bob Eschelman

The instrument panel of the TF was quite striking with its octagon-shaped bezels.

Model	TC	TD	TF1250	TF1500
Engine	4 cyl	4 cyl	4 cyl	4 cyl
Capacity	1250cc	1250cc	1250cc	1466cc
Bore & Stroke	66.5x90	66.5x90	66.5x90	72x90
Compression Ratio	-	-	8.0:1	8.3:1
HP	54@5200	54@5200	57@5500	63@5000
Torque	64@2600	64@2600	65@3000	76@3000
Wheelbase	94in	-	-	-
OA Length	139.5in	145in	147.0in	-
OA Width	56in	58.6in	59.7in	-
OA Height	53in	53in	52.5in	-
Weight	1,735lb	1,930lb	1,930lb	-
Tires	5.50x15	-	-	-
Top Speed	75mph	80mph	80 (R&T)	85 (R&T)

The optional non-stock wire wheels of the TF.

Engine detail from the carburetor side.

⬡3

MGA

When the MGA was introduced in 1955, it brought the MG Car Company right into the 20th century. Granted, the T-series cars were fun and exuded a certain charm, but they were far from aerodynamic in a world that was putting increasing emphasis on how a car moved through the air. And they lacked the amenities of modern motoring. The MGA solved many of those problems.

The A was based on another MG record-breaking car; EX.179. This car had all the external features of the production car as well as many of the internals. EX.179 and the production MGA both used 1489cc inline pushrod four-cylinder engines. In the EX.179 it was rated at 82hp, while in the production car it was rated at 68hp. The difference may be attributed to the compression ratio, which was 9.4:1 in EX.179 and 8.3:1 in the A.

A 1962 MGA 1600 Mark II Coupe owned by Jonathan A. Stein. *L. Hemmings, courtesy of* Automobile Quarterly

According to *Safety Fast*, the MG Car Club magazine: "The basic lines of the new body already existed, in the form of the special 'TD' which Syd Enever had built for George Phillips to drive at LeMans in 1951. The chassis frame, too, had been tested—first in the EX.175 development car based on the Phillips LeMans model, and later in the EX.179 record-breaker. As for the engine—there was the splendid new B.M.C. 'B' type power unit, already proving its worth in the 'ZA' Magnette saloon [sedan]. So a batch of prototypes was built and tested to the limit, including competing in the LeMans 24-Hours and Tourist Trophy races of 1955. In August of that year the new car went into full production and the following month it was announced to the public as the M.G. Series 'MGA'—thus making a fresh start at the beginning of the alphabet after thirty years of rather confusing type-letters and numbers."

The Autocar published the first road test of the new A in September 1955 and called it

When Lance Babbitt had his MGA 1500 repainted, he chose British Racing Green, even though the color wasn't originally available for the car. He drives it every day.

From the top, the MGA's passenger compartment is cozy. The optional wood steering wheel telescoped on its column.

"a worthy successor to the famous and well-loved T-types, incorporating many lessons learned in racing. At any price it is a desirable car for normal road use, yet still suitable for competition in the 1,500 c.c. class."

Safety Fast admitted that the sleek shape of the new MG probably upset the traditionalists, but its advantages couldn't be ignored. It was not only more modern that the TF it replaced, it was more comfortable, handled better, and also had a modest trunk.

In the United States, *Car Life*'s test in September 1956 called the MGA "a beautifully handling, handsome and ruggedly made little car which will serve as inexpensive and highly practical transportation within the obvious limitations of size and riding comfort."

A team of MGA sports prototypes raced at Le Mans in 1955, finishing twelfth and seventeenth overall. But the basic chassis for what was to become the MGA was designed for the 1951 Le Mans race. According to the British magazine *Thoroughbred & Classic Cars*, this chassis placed the driver and passenger lower in the cockpit than with the T-Types. The chassis was ready early in 1952. John Thornley was appointed General Manager of the MG Car Company in 1952 and championed the new chassis and car to the BMC executives. Leonard Lord rejected it, allegedly because he didn't want competition for the

The rear view of the 1500 shows how one can distinguish it from later MGAs: the single unit taillight lenses. BMC used these same taillight lenses on other vehicles as well, making maximum use of the parts bin.

The MGA grille retained the vertical slats of previous MGs, but in a more square format. The grille badge has been replaced.

Austin-Healey. So when a new MG model was introduced in 1953, it was the TF rather than the more modern MGA.

Eventually, though, Lord relented and the MGA was slated for production. The car was designed by Syd Enever with encouragement from John Thornley. Its name was proper, because MG had finally finished its first run through the alphabet with the Z-Type Magnette sedan. It was time for a new beginning.

While the Austin-Healey 3000 offered buyers brute power (at a price), the MGA's power was more modest, only 68hp at 5,800rpm. It was with handling that the MGA achieved a level of equality. The independent front suspension was not unlike that in the TD and TF, with double A-arms, lever

Instrument panel and original steering wheel of the MGA 1500.

This ad for the MGA 1600 combined it with the Bugeye Sprite and Austin-Healey 3000. With the top, middle, and bottom of the price spectrum covered, BMC had control of the sports car market. *Collection of the author*

shock absorbers and coil springs. The beam rear axle was suspended by semielliptic leaf springs and tubular shocks.

On the 1500 MGA, the brakes were drums all around, but on the 1600 and 1600 Mark II, discs were added to the front. On the more exciting Twin Cam, four-wheel disc brakes were installed.

The 1489cc engine in the MGA was derived from the BMC B-type engine. With a bore and stroke of 2.875 by 3.5in, the four-banger was just slightly larger than

This silhouetted MGA 1600 Mark II shows its aerodynamic profile.

the XPEG engine it replaced but delivered five more horses.

The engine drove the rear wheels through a four-speed transmission with synchromesh on the top three gears only. Many drivers who never mastered the art of double clutching cursed that gearbox because they usually had to come to a complete stop before shifting into first every time.

Car Life reported that "the car is a do-it-yourself dream, every part being easily accessible and readily demountable. Best of all, vir-

This shot shows the unique recessed grille of the 1600 Mark II.

tually every nut and bolt is standardized with 'Unified' or American National Fine threads and bolt heads are made to standard American hexagon wrench sizes."

Originally, the MGA came only as a soft-top convertible. Side screens were fitted, with a hinged flap at the bottom to reach out to pay tolls. This lower flap was also useful for getting into the car. The MGA was designed without exterior door handles; to enter you lifted up the bottom section of the side screen and reached inside and pulled a cord which opened the door. But then the MGA was built and sold in an era when double and triple-locking all your possessions wasn't necessary. However, these side curtains never offered ideal weather protection. As they got older, spaces grew between the cur-

tains and the windshield frame—spaces of as much as 2in.

Buyers leapt at the opportunity to buy the MGA, and the model racked up a grand total of over 100,000 sales in its seven-year life. The 1500 was built from August 1955 to May 1959, when it was replaced by the 1600. But there was a more potent version of the "A" available in the interim.

MGA Twin Cam

In April 1958, MG began building the Twin Cam version of the MGA. Physically, the Twin Cam had center-lock disc wheels with four-wheel disc brakes installed behind them. A small "Twin Cam" badge, located next to the air holes on the top of the hood, was the only external identification.

Under the hood, though, was a potent engine that proved to be difficult to keep in a good state of tune, but when it was properly maintained and tuned could lay a streak of rubber in all four gears. To quote Wilson McComb, "The twin-ohc engine had a cross-flow cylinder head in aluminum alloy, larger SU carburetors were used, and the bottom end was generally sturdier than on the pushrod unit. Although the 88.9mm stroke of the experimental 1489cc engine had been retained, the bore was increased to 75.4mm to give a capacity of 1588cc, thus making better use of the 1600cc class that had now become popular in competition and the power output was 108hp at 6700rpm. . . . The effect of the new engine was impressive."

The tonneau cover was a nice feature. It protected the seats from sun or rain with the top down, or opened halfway, it offered the driver some protection from the cold and gave a more aerodynamic surface.

Next page
This Hambro ad from the July 1956 *Road & Track* combines the "entirely new MGA: The safest, fastest MG ever engineered!" with the Austin-Healey 100. *Collection of the author*

40

2
Great New Challengers...

THE ENTIRELY NEW — MG A

The safest, fastest MG ever engineered!

THE NEW 1956

Austin-Healey
100

Featuring a new four-speed gearbox with overdrive!

Products of BMC — Makers of **MG, AUSTIN-HEALEY, MAGNETTE, MORRIS, AUSTIN & RILEY CARS.** *Represented in the United States by —* **hambro**

But even McComb admitted that "the very high compression engine (9.9:1) called for a fuel of at least 100 octane rating, which was not generally available at the time. The mixture strength, and even the ignition timing had to be exactly right."

The Twin Cams were giving MG a bad name in the United States. While the base MGA was a dream, the Twin Cam was a nightmare. It was discontinued in April 1960 after only 2,111 had been built in it's two years of production.

According to former *Automobile Quarterly* editor Don Vorderman, the inherent problem with the Twin Cam was in the pistons, and owner Terry Kozo agrees. The tops of the pistons are raised in a wedge shape. While this shape made for a higher compression ratio, it also led to holed out pistons when a valve would contact the piston on an

The taillights were repositioned from the fenders to just under the trunk lid.

A 1959 ad for the MGA. *Automobile Quarterly*

uphill run. Flat-topped pistons eliminate the problem. While the compression ratio is reduced slightly, the life of the pistons is extended immeasurably, and makes the Twin Cam a certain winner in 1990s vintage races.

MGA 1600

After the decline of the Twin Cam, MG introduced a new MGA in July 1959, with a slightly larger engine. The MGA 1600 had a 1588cc engine rated at 80hp and was built

Engine heat exhaust vent detail from the Mark II.

Jonathan A. Stein's 1962 MGA 1600 Mark II
Coupe. *L. Hemmings, courtesy of* Automobile
Quarterly

from May 1959 to April 1961. The 1600 also wore MG's first (not counting the Twin Cam) disc brakes (up front). A few spare Twin Cam chassis were used with 1589 engines, creating the 1600 De Luxe.

The 1600 was distinguishable from the 1500 by a discreet "1600" badge near the oval hood air exhausts and by two-piece taillights. Other small improvements to make the 1600 more hospitable were a better hood, aluminum-framed sliding sidescreens instead of the plastic lift-up style, parking lamps, and a revised pedal layout.

Speaking of pedals, one feature enjoyed by many MGA owners who found themselves passengers in another MGA was the pedal linkages. Since the MGA was British (even though 70-80 percent were exported to the United States) the pedal linkages were on the right side of the chassis. To accommodate left-hand drive, the linkages came through the firewall on the right side, then connected

This fully restored dash is as close to what the original dash looked like as is possible.

The 100,000th MGA, a 1600 Mark II roadster, was displayed on the MG stand at the 1962 New York Auto Show. It had special gold paint, white carpeting, and special trim details.

When BMC introduced the MGA 1600 in July 1959, it was "Safety Fast" with a more powerful engine and solid disc brakes. *Collection of the author*

over to the pedals on the left. Knowledgeable passengers could work the pedals and put a scare into the person behind the wheel.

MGA 1600 MKII

The ultimate street MGA was the 1600 Mark II, built from April 1961 to June 1962. The Mark II developed 90hp at 5500rpm from its 1622cc engine. The extra ccs and the extra power made a big difference. For example, you could go from 0 to 60mph in just 13.8 seconds. The car had an honest top

Coupe versions had these tasteful exterior door handles.

Above and right
MGA Twin Cam with the top up. It's still a nice-looking car. Owner: Terry Kozo

speed in the low 90s. While the engine was larger internally, externally its dimensions were almost identical to previous engines. The engine was as easy to service and maintain as earlier engines as well, making the Mark II a do-it-yourselfer's delight.

This engine wasn't simply a re-boring of the 1588cc engine. It had a new cylinder block, new pistons, new connecting rods, new crankshaft, new and lighter flywheel, new cylinder head with larger valves and stronger springs, and a new ribbed casing for the gearbox.

Following the "Safety Fast" motto, the Mark II also stopped well. With 11in Lockheed disc brakes up front and 10in drums at the rear, the Mark II may have been over-braked, but it gave the drivers a lot of confidence.

Inside, any MGA fan would recognize the controls; there were no changes. With the horn button mounted in the center of the dash and a radio panel on the right side, all MGAs were identical.

All MGA engine compartments, except for the Twin Cam, were virtually identical. The difference was in the engine displacement. This is the 1600 Mark II with the 1622cc engine..

The Mark II had a unique grille which distinguished it from earlier MGAs. The frame was identical to earlier cars, but the vertical slats were recessed, giving the grille a three-dimensional effect that earlier (and later) MGs didn't have. While MG historian Wilson McComb calls the grille design "not very inspired," owners liked it. Taillight design as well was changed. Instead of being positioned vertically on the trailing edge of the rear fenders, the taillights were mounted horizontally inboard.

In addition, the side windows were a definite improvement. Gone were the old celluloid and fabric curtains. In their place were framed sliding plexiglass windows that offered considerably more weather protection. The top was manually operated and stowed behind the seats. A tonneau cover was supplied for when the driver wanted to maintain top-down motoring.

Some 1622 engines were installed in spare Twin Cam chassis, creating the MGA 1600 Mark II De Luxe. A pair of De Luxe coupes finished first and second in class at Sebring, and Don Morley won his class in the 1962 Monte Carlo Rally with a 1600 Mark II coupe.

One mark that the Mark II set for the MG Car Company was in the spring of 1962 when the 100,000th MGA rolled off the Abingdon assembly line. This car was painted a metallic gold with a white interior and was featured on the MG stand at the New York Auto Show in April.

But the MGA 1600 Mark II wasn't to last long. In 1962 it was replaced by the MGB, which was a far more civilized car.

Coupe Versions

Although MGAs were available with removable hardtops, both from the factory and the numerous aftermarket suppliers, the

MGA instruments included, from left, a tachometer, speedometer, fuel, and oil pressure/battery gauges. The grille conceals a speaker for the optional radio, which would be fitted at right. Under the grille is the horn button.

first fixed-head coupe was introduced in 1956 at the London Motor Show. The sleek hardtop had glass side windows and exterior door handles. The smoother lines of the fixed-head coupe allowed the MGA to reach 102mph in test. The coupe was available in all versions of the "A," including the Twin Cam. The most popular was the 1500, with 6,272 produced, followed by the 1600 (2,771), 1600 Mark II (521), and Twin Cam (323). In total, just under 10,000 coupes were built.

The identification on the engine heat exhaust outlet gives away the secret of what's under the hood.

Terry Kozo's Twin Cam MGA.

	MGA 1600	MGA 1600	MGA Twin Cam	MGA MkII
Engine	1489cc	1588cc	1622cc	1588cc
C.R.	8.3:1	8.3:1	8.9:1	9.9:1
BHP	68@5500	79.5@5600	90@5500	108@6700
Torque	77.4@3500	87@3800	97@4000	104@4500
Tires	5.60X15	5.60x15	5.60X15	5.90X15
WB	94.0 in	94.0 in	94.0 in	94.0 in.
OAL	156.0 in	-	-	156.0 in.
OAW	58 in	-	-	58 in.
OAHgt	50 in	-	-	50 in.
Weight	-	2,072 lb	2185 lb.	-
0-60	14.2 sec	12.6 sec.	-	-
0-100	-	-	-	38.1 sec.
Top Speed	98 mph	96 mph	105 mph	108 mph
Price	$2,200	$2,599	-	-
Total built	58,750	31,501	8,719	2,111

The MGA Twin Cam engine, 1588cc, 108hp at 6700rpm. Only 2,111 were built, but some engines, chassis, and wheels were fitted to 1500 and 1600 Deluxes.

⑧

MGB, MGB/GT, & MGC

The MGB was the best selling sports car of all time, not counting the Corvette. Of course, you have to count the 'Vette, with its sales of over one million, but the MGB's half million sales were nothing to sneeze at.

In 1962, MG finally entered the modern age with the MGB after dabbling with roll-up windows and the hardtop coupe MGA. The MGB would also prove to be MG's last gasp, although a six-cylinder-engined model would be offered (the MGC) and every resurrection of the marque to date sees an MGB-type vehicle wearing the "Sacred Octagon."

With the MGA's introduction delayed from the early 1950s until 1955, work began on its replacement almost immediately. Syd Enever was the chief engineer at MG responsible for the development of the B. John Thornley was his boss as general manager of the MG Car Company from 1952 until 1969.

Thornley said in 1957, "My imagination was fired by seeing a trio of Aston Martin DB2/4 coupes competing in a production car race at Silverstone. I can remember seeing the three of them, side by side, on the track, to this day. I thought 'that's the shape our new car ought to be.'" So the B was to be a hardtop from the beginning, although it originally appeared as a roadster.

With that original concept in mind, Enever assigned MG's chief body engineer, Jim O'Neill, to design a coupe derived form the EX181 record breaking car. The design was given the code EX205/1.

A design for the new MG was also prepared by Pietro Frua in Turin, Italy. Frua had gained his reputation with the Maserati Mistral and would eventually design similar cars on AC and other chassis. But his MG was completely different for Frua, with a Lancia-type front end and side and rear sections that were a definite inspiration for the final MGB shape. But, according to author Jonathan Wood, "It did not meet with general approval,

Joyce Tucker's 1968 MGB. *Mike Mueller*

MG brought out the MGB in 1962 with a 1798cc four-cylinder engine rated at 95hp, roll-up windows, and lockable doors. By 1968, when Joyce Tucker's car was built, a fully synchronized four-speed transmission was finally available. An automatic became optional in mid-1975. Wire wheels were another option. In all, MG sold 512,880 MGBs. Owner: Joyce Tucker. *Mike Mueller*

Right
In 1963, the early "classic" MGB had chrome bumpers, wire wheels, and whitewall tires. It was a "Product of the British Motor Corporation." Later versions would claim different parentage. *Collection of the author*

Busier bee in her bonnet.

Her windows wind up. And down.

More room in her lockable boot.

All new from stem to stern.

Candid advice to the gal who has accepted an invitation to share a test ride in the new MGB for '63. If he wants to bet that your hairdo will stay done, don't bet. He'll simply wind up the windows. If he says that he can easily top a 100, he's right. Don't worry. Remember, the MG is the "Safety-fast" car. When he balks at letting you drive, don't argue. Let him have his fun. Just smile to yourself and enjoy all the luxurious passenger conveniences instead. After all your BMC dealer is an understanding guy. He'll be glad to arrange a test-drive just for you. Warning: Once in, you won't want out.

Product of The British Motor Corporation Ltd., makers of MG, Austin Healey, Sprite, Morris and Austin cars. Represented in the United States by Hambro Automotive Corporation, 27 West 57th Street, New York 19, N.Y.

which is perhaps a polite way of putting it! Not only was it a weighty car with poor performance—which was in any case incidental because it was a styling exercise—it also looked heavy."

Eventually, the Frua car was destroyed because it had been brought to England on an import bond which meant no duty had been paid on it.

In 1958, a wooden mock-up of a full-scale monocoque body took shape. This coupe was designed by Don Hayter, who just

By 1970, when Pete Ernst's car was built, the MGB had lost its chrome grille and gained headrests. This car is totally original, with optional fog lights and mirrors. The only items not on the original car are the tires, which were replaced by the original owner. Owner: Pete Ernst

The only damage to this well-maintained 1970 MGB is a small ding in the grille surround.

Unfortunately, the replacement was not a perfect match, so it wasn't used.

happened to also be on the Aston Martin team responsible for designing the DB2/4 that originally drew John Thornley's admiration. Hayter's design was very MGB-like, but used an MGA chassis and an MGA 1600 Mark II grille. The consensus was that the design was close to what was wanted, but it wasn't there yet.

Hayter then "took a clean sheet of paper" and started all over. He remembered, "I took a new EX number, 214, and 214/1 was drawn quarter-scale straight on to the paper which I then gave to Harry Herring, our modelmaker, and that was the MGB all in one go." He completed the drawing on June 19, 1958. Thornley took Herring's model to BMC head-

In profile, the MGB doesn't have the flowing lines of the MGA, but it was as aerodynamic and obvi-ously sold more. The profile doesn't lose anything with the top up.

quarters and received approval to build a full-size prototype. At that time it also received its corporate ADO23 project number.

The prototype body was built at Morris Bodies, and the car was assembled at Abingdon. It had a coil spring rear axle—eventually abandoned—and an MGA 1588cc engine. Three prototypes were built, followed by eight pre-production cars. The pre-production cars used a dash that was also designed by Hayter.

The B's mechanical side was developed under the leadership of Terry Mitchell, with Roy Brocklehurst assisting. After experimenting with different rear suspensions, they abandoned an independent rear because of cost, then tried a live axle with coil springs and a Watts linkage, then a Panhard rod.

By 1971, the MGB had traded its wire wheels for Rostyle wheels that predicted the coming trend to mag-style and aluminum wheels. *Collection of the author*

Nothing worked within the tight budget constraints so they returned to the leaf spring rear of the MGA, which required a lengthening of the body.

For the engine in the production car, MG used the latest BMC B-series inline four, with a 1798cc capacity and developing 95hp. Unlike its predecessor, which was powered by four different engines during its body life, the MGB engine remained the same through the life of the car, albeit with slight modifications to comply with emerging emissions requirements. As reported in *Thoroughbred & Classic Cars*, "The most notable shift was from a three-bearing to a five-bearing crankshaft in 1964. The early 'banjo-type' axle was dropped in favor of a stronger tube-type, pull-type door handles were replaced by safer, pushbutton ones in early 1965 and an all-new gearbox with [finally!] synchromesh on first appeared in late 1967."

Dimensionally, the MGB was 3in shorter than the A, yet was 2-1/2in wider, thanks to its monocoque construction. It had a larger trunk and there was even room for two children to sit behind the front seats.

Left
This view shows the seating capacity.

The MGB dash was padded and had full instrumentation.

Beginning in 1968, all MGs sold in the United States had to conform to Federal safety standards. While requiring the manufacturers to crash-test examples of each model, each car also was modified to conform to new regulations. U.S. versions of the "B" had new dashes, with deep foam padding covered with black leatherette cloth. The padding eliminated the glove box.

Toggle switches, which were located all over the dash, were replaced by rockers to eliminate any possibility of injury by the "second collision" of driver/passenger with the dash. Stalk switches for turn signals, horn, headlights and wipers were mounted on the steering column, which was collapsible. An additional safety feature was a dual braking system with twin master cylinders. And the windshield was constructed of high-impact laminated glass. Two-speed wipers were required on all models, but they were already standard on the MGB and MGC.

MGB/GT

A fixed-head (hardtop) coupe version of the MGB was introduced in October

MGB power came from a 1798cc four-cylinder engine with dual downdraft SU carburetors. This engine is original and has not been repainted.

Right
By 1976, the MGB Roadster had lost its chrome bumpers to big black "rubber baby buggy bumpers" that were the result of federal 5mph impact regulations. *Collection of the author*

MGB presents the world's biggest sunroof.

A super sunroof: a fully-convertible top that opens wide to let the sunshine in. It's standard equipment on every 1976 MGB. Along with the classic look and wide-open performance that have made MG famous for 50 years as one of the world's great sports car bargains.

MGB holds the Class E Championship in the Sports Car Club of America's national competition, as it has for four of the last five years.

Performance like this can't be faked: you can't fool a finish line with a flashy paint job or a fancy name. MGB's authentic sports car performance and crisp handling grow naturally out of standard equipment like radial tires, front disc brakes, short-throw, four-speed stick shift, rack and pinion steering and a race-proven 1798 cc engine.

If what you're driving makes you forget what fun is, take one MGB, fast. For the name of your nearest MG dealer, call these toll-free numbers: (800) 447-4700, or, in Illinois, (800) 322-4400.

BRITISH LEYLAND MOTORS INC. LEONIA, NEW JERSEY 07605

MGB the wide-open sports car.

1965. The B/GT was a beautiful example of the MGB.

Art Smith, who owns both an MGTC and an MGB/GT, noted that when the cars are parked together and the TC's top is raised, the slope of the rear window over the fuel tank in the TC is almost identical to that of the slope of the rear window of the MGB/GT.

With the 1965 cars came a new five-bearing crankshaft that offered smoother running at high speeds. The new crankshaft was a result of modifications to the engine for the Austin 1800 sedan.

The MGB/GT was preceded by a customized version of the MGB called the Berlinette MGB 1800, designed by Jacques Coune of Brussels, Belgium. The Berlinette was constructed of metal from the grille to

Above and right
In 1980, the last year of MGB production, MG built the LE, or Limited Edition, model. It had Rostyle wheels, special decals, a special front spoiler, and the less powerful engine. Owner: Bob Hulshouser

the rear of the doors, with the rest of the body being built of fiberglass.

One feature the GT version gave the MGB was added carrying capacity. According to MGB historians Jonathan Wood and Lionel Burrell, the storage area was 38in wide and 30in from the back of the rear seats to the rear of the car. With the rear seats lowered, that capacity became 38in square.

The GT used the same engine as the roadster, with the primary differences being in the chassis and suspension. The GT, for

MGB
LIMITED EDITION

UNLIMITED FUN.

Here are the classic lines and quick response that have made MGB America's best-selling convertible. Here is the agility of rack and pinion steering, short-throw four-speed stick, and the stopping power of front disc brakes. And now it's all enhanced by the striking design and accessories of the Limited Edition, available only in black accented by dramatic silver striping. The Limited Edition comes with distinctive cast-alloy wheels and wide-profile tires. There are performance features like a front air dam and a padded, smaller diameter racing-type steering wheel for quicker response. There is a sturdy luggage rack, coco mats and an official Limited Edition plaque on the dashboard. The edition is Limited. The fun isn't. For the name of your nearest MG dealer, call toll-free: (800) 447-4700. In Illinois: (800) 322-4400.

Jaguar Rover Triumph Inc. Leonia, N.J. 07605.

Special Limited Edition Plaque.   Sturdy luggage rack.   Padded racing-type wheel.   Front air dam.

example, used a Salisbury-type rear axle as opposed to the "Banjo-type" rear axle on the roadster, which was derived from the MGA's.

In addition, the GT had a stiffer rear suspension because of the extra weight in the rear. Since this stiffer suspension increased over-

Previous page
The Limited Edition MGB LE was advertised as "Unlimited Fun." In reality, despite a nice set of options and special trim pieces, the LE was one of the tamest MGBs, since it appeared at the height of the reduced emissions/reduced power cycle. *Collection of the author*

US Federal safety regulations essentially killed the MGB's classic grille, replacing it with a "rubber baby buggy bumper" version that was allegedly safer.

steer, an anti-roll bar was added to the front. Overall, the GT weighed about 250lb more than the roadster.

This added weight cut into the performance. Where the roadster could go from 0-60 mph in 12.6 seconds, according to *Motor*, the GT took about .6 seconds longer. Top speed was about the same with both cars, primarily because of the aerodynamic efficiency of the GT.

By May 1971, 250,000 MGBs had been built, more than double the production total of the MGA. Cars built to 1972 specifications had rocker switches on the dash. Rubber inserts on the bumper overriders were added

for the American market, but eventually became standard for all MGBs because of the importance of that market.

By the 1975 model year, the rubber inserts were replaced by large polyurethane bumpers. In accordance with American federal safety regulations, they were required not to deform in a 5mph frontal impact. The MGB also lost its traditional vertical-slatted "MG" grille, gained 70lb in weight, and 5in in length. Air injector pumps were added to the engine to reduce emissions. This addition was a popular move early in emissions compliance. Later, fuel injection and computer-controlled fuel metering systems would make

The LE's dash contained full instrumentation, heater vents, and a radio.

air pumps unnecessary. But they would also suck power from the engines.

In 1979, a Limited Edition version of the MGB was offered for U.S. customers. All LE cars were black with silver stripes and special-design alloy wheels. Other equipment added to "LE" models included a front spoiler, leather-wrapped steering wheel, chrome luggage rack, and a special dash plaque signifying that the vehicle was, indeed, an LE.

In January 1980, the 500,000th MGB, a roadster, was built. But the decision had already been made to cease MG production. Wood and Burrell described the end thusly:

"By the summer of 1979, [British Leyland] Cars' problem of deteriorating finances was further exacerbated by the rising value of the pound; a trend that had started at the beginning of 1979 and accelerated with the Conservative election victory in May. The situation became so serious that, in July, Edwardes and his top management team met at Ye Olde Bell, Hurley, Berkshire, to try to resolve the problem. An outcome of this meeting was the decision that the BL workforce would have to be cut by a further 25,000. The Triumph factory at Canley would have to close while MG production at Abingdon would also have to cease and with it the MGB. Such was the high value of the

The far-more-complicated engine of the 1980 MGB with its air pump to reduce emissions and single Zenith carburetor. Horsepower was significantly less that the 95hp of the original.

The 1971 MGB/GT is virtually identical to the roadster, except for the hardtop. Owner: Art King

The 1971 MGB/GT.

pound against the dollar that, in the summer of 1979, BL calculated it was losing £900 on every MGB it sold in America."

The last MGB body was built by Pressed Steel at Stratton St. Margaret on October 2, 1980. On October 22, it reached the end of the line at Abingdon. With it, MG also reached the end of the same line.

That vehicle ultimately made it to the United States, by far the largest market for MGBs. It was purchased by Henry Ford II and placed in the Henry Ford Museum and Greenfield Village. In 1995, the "Last MG Imported to the United States" joined "The First MG Imported to the United States" in the Gast Classic Motorcars Museum in Strasburg, Pennsylvania.

	MGB Mark I
Years built	1962-67
Wheelbase	91.0in
OAL	153.2in
OAW	59.9in
OAH	49.4in
Max speed	103mph
0-60mph	12.2sec
Total built	115,898
To USA	71,722

MGC

Early in 1968, BMC added the MGC to its line in the United States. The car had been

Some cars can boast of styling. Others can take pleasure in possessing an elusive quality called "style". But few cars can make a claim on both. Happily, the 1973 MGB/GT can. Motor Trend, in fact, has called the MGB/GT "the most civilized MG ever built". But style and styling isn't all there is to a genuine Grand Touring sports car. Beneath the MGB/GT's exterior can be found a pure sports car. One that can take the uncertainty out of every curve and eats up a stretch of straightaway with gusto. It's all in the rack and pinion steering, the proven suspension system and the ruggedness of the track-tested engine. Slip into an MGB/GT and you'll experience a GT with a style all its own.

This 1973 MGB/GT brochure promoted the car's sophistication. Note the rubber inserts on the bumper overriders that would "grow" to cover the whole bumper in a few years. *Collection of the author*

With the hatch closed, the MGB/GT looked very much like any other hatchback coupe or sedan.

With it opened, access to the rear storage area was improved. Owner: Art King

introduced the year before at the London Motor Show, and while it sort of looked like the MGB, it was really a different car.

The most obvious physical differences between the "B" and "C" were a hood bulge and larger wheels and tires. The hood bulge was to accommodate a new 2912cc inline six engine; the wheels and tires were to get the extra power to the road.

According to *Safety Fast*, "There was ample length under the bonnet for the three-liter engine, but the bonnet top had to be modified to take the taller unit, resulting in the 'power bulge.'" While the engine had essentially the same internal dimensions as the BMC C-series engine used in the Austin-Healey 3000, it was, in fact, an entirely new unit. It was smaller in external size, lighter in weight, and carried seven main bearings instead of five. But even though it was smaller, it was taller, so a hood bulge was needed for clearance. This engine, in what was essentially the MGB, gave, according to *Safety Fast*, "all the superb handling and maneuverability of the 'MGB' with all the performance of the Healey 3000."

The 2912cc inline six had a 9.0:1 compression ratio and was rated at 150hp at 5250rpm, with torque rated at 174lb/ft at 3500rpm. A four-speed all-synchromesh transmission was standard, with a two-speed Borg-Warner automatic available as an option. The automatic at the same time became an option on the MGB.

Stuart Seager, editor of *Safety Fast*, tested an MGC against a "B" in 1967. While the "B" went from 0-60 in 11.8 seconds, the "C" took just 9.8 seconds; 0-to-90 took 35 seconds in the "B" and 20.1 seconds in the "C." Top speed was 126 in the "C" versus 107 in the "B." Granted, *Safety Fast* was the MG Car Club publication, but it was also a BMC publica-

tion, so Seager's opinion that "the tremendous acceleration of the MGC is a real joy to use," may have been slightly prejudiced. In comparing the automatic with the manual gearbox, Seager recorded identical times over the quarter mile.

While the 3-liter MGC was nominally a great product for MG, it proved to be the undoing of the relationship between Donald Healey and BMC. Geoff Healey wrote in *Austin Healey: The Story of the Big Healeys*:

The original concept of ADO51 and 52 [the Austin-Healey and MG prototype numbers, respectively] as a common MG-Austin Healey sports car had a good deal of merit, but the final version was a great disappointment to all concerned. After a somewhat confused origin in 1960, it was eventually announced, as the MGC, in 1967. 56 percent of the new six-cylinder's weight, with its seven main bearings, was centered on the front wheels. Handling was poor, with very strong understeering characteristics. Des-pite using the same bore and stroke as the Healey 3000 engine, the maximum power was down and the low

The MGB/GT had vestigial rear seats that folded down to increase luggage capacity.

speed torque very poor. . . .

BMC tried very hard to persuade [Donald Healey] to agree to his name being used on ADO51. A number of attempts were made to upgrade the car to a form that was acceptable, but all left with the feeling that the one-piece classic design of the MGB had been butchered to produce a medi-ocre sports car. The expensive tooling of the MGB body/chassis assembly (in contrast to the low-cost tooling of the Austin Healey) inhibited any fundamental alterations or improvements. I spent a lot of time with Syd Enever on the project, and though he did everything possible to make a success of it, I felt that he realized that it was not the way to go. Perhaps if DMH had agreed to his name

The MGC could be differentiated from the MGB by the hood bulge, necessary to cover the inline six engine. In two years, just 8,999 MGCs were built, about half roadsters and half GTs.

The slope of the rear hatch is strangely similar to that of the MG TC with the top up.

going on the car, extra development funds might have been made available and it might ultimately have been a success. As things turned out, however, DMH was undoubtedly right to refuse to have his name connected with this unsuccessful vehicle."

Total MGC roadster production from 1967 to 1969 was 4,542 vehicles; 2,483 were delivered to the United States, 1,403 in England, and 656 in the rest of the world. Approximately the same number of MGC GTs were built—4,457.

Under the hood, the MGC carried a 2912cc (nominally 3-liter) inline six that was rated at 145hp.

Several chrome parts have been added.

⑧

MG Midget

The British Motor Corporation was not unlike almost any other automobile manufacturer in the 1960s. If it could make a few extra dollars (or pounds sterling) by badge engineering an existing vehicle, then who was the loser? Thus was the modern variation of the MG Midget created in mid-1961 as an offshoot of the Mark II Austin Healey Sprite.

The Sprite began its life back in 1958 as the much-loved Bugeye (or Frogeye in England) version. Here was a car that was cuter than the Neon thinks it is, with a curious bug-eye look thanks to raised headlights that were placed up there to comply with minimum headlight height requirement laws. The original Sprite was powered by the 948cc BMC "A" engine delivering 52hp at 3300rpm. The Sprite was cute, sexy in an odd way, and offered sports car-like performance for a very low price, around $1500-$1700.

But it had its problems. In the original version, trunk access was difficult without a true trunk opening (access to the luggage compartment was, like in many Corvettes, from behind the seats). It was reasonably weather-tight with its side curtains, but as with all side-curtained cars, those could also be quite leaky after a while, making the car decidedly non-weatherproof.

The Sprite also had a very good competition record, being driven by an assortment of drivers that included Stirling Moss, Pat Moss, and Steve McQueen, among others.

BMC built almost 49,000 Bugeye Sprites before it introduced the Mark II version in May 1961. Along with the Mark II Sprite, BMC resurrected a revered name from MG's history, the MG Midget. While the cars were

The MG Midget was a more refined badge-engineered version of he Austin-Healey Sprite. This British Racing Green Mark II has chrome wire wheels, the classic chrome MG grille with vertical slats, wind-up windows, and leather seats. Performance was modest with the Mark I's original 948cc four-cylinder BMC "A" engine, but handling and panache were on a par with the more powerful sports cars. Owner: Bernie Rapaport. *Dave Gooley*

certainly better-designed than the Bugeye, they both lacked the charm and panache that the little original Sprite had.

The Midget Mark I (although it wasn't known as the Mark I when it was introduced) was powered by the 948cc engine, now developing 46.4hp at 5500rpm, thanks to larger SU carburetors. It was fairly easy to distinguish the Midget from the Sprite (collectively they were known as Spridgets); the Sprite had

This is a window. It rolls up and down.

This is an MG midget. It rolls forward...fast.

And this is a word to anyone who's looking for a pure sports car for about $2,000. Buy a Midget. Whether you race it (Class G or H) or get your kicks from roaming the countryside, this hot little package will add spice to the sport. Four-speed gearbox, twin-carb power, 8¼" disc brakes up front, 7" drums in rear, 1098 cc. MG Engine. Zero to 60 in less than 16 seconds. In addition to wind-up windows, the new Midget has a redesigned fascia, locking doors and glove compartment and new improved rear suspension. Same trim lines. Same meticulous detail. Drive one...soon.

MG MIDGET

JUNE 1964

MG introduced the Midget in 1961. By 1964, when this ad ran, it still had its chrome grille, wire wheels, and had gained "roll up and down" windows combined with a price of about $2,000. *Collection of the author*

an eggcrate grille while the Midget had a grille that somewhat mimicked traditional MG grilles with vertical chrome slats. In BMC nomenclature, it was the GAN.1.

Creature comforts in the Midget were a definite improvement over the original Sprite (and, for that matter, the MGA 1600 then on the market). It had a lockable trunk with a true trunk cover, and drum brakes on all four wheels, and removable sidescreens. *Motor Trend* tested a Midget in October 1962 and recorded a 0-60 time of 20.0 seconds, a quarter-mile time of 23.2 seconds, and fuel economy ratings of 27.3 to 34.6mpg.

Technical Editor Jim Wright, who wrote the review combined with one of the 1600

Nine right-hand-drive Midgets on the assembly line at Abingdon. *Collection of the author*

The MG Midget was never more than a two-seater. Cozy for long-legged drivers and passengers, it was still full of fun for all. *Dave Gooley*

Mark II, said "after spending quite a bit of time in both cars we personally prefer the Midget. While it isn't as fast as the Mk II, we found that pound for pound and inch for inch it offers a shade more performance and a whale of a lot more fun. For another thing, it is quite a bit cheaper, initially, and much, much more economical to operate. Besides that, it comes closest to having the certain indefinable something that made the TC the car that it was."

A later version of the Mark I Midget (GAN.2) added disc front brakes, a carpeted floor, and a more powerful 1098cc engine that delivered 55hp at 5500rpm.

True modernity came to Midgetdom in 1964 with the Midget Mark II (GAN.3). This iteration kept the 1098cc engine, but with a stiffer crankshaft and a new cylinder head with larger valves, the engine now developed

At the end of a winding road is where you would expect to see the MG Midget. The cute, friendly Midget offered excellent handling for its time in a small modern sports car. It was the Mazda Miata of its era, with seating for two, a modest trunk, a slick four-speed gearbox and *de rigeur* wire wheels. *Dave Gooley*

From this angle, the Midget's similarity to the larger MGB is evident. The two cars were vastly different, both in interior space and performance, but they bore a family resemblance that modern brand designers are trying to achieve. *Dave Gooley*

MG Midget four-cylinder engines ranged from the 948cc 52hp BMC "A" of the Mark I through the 1098cc 55hp second generation Mark I, to the 65hp 1275cc unit in the Mark III, to the 1491cc unit of the Mark IV GAN.6, that developed 65hp. In total, almost 225,000 MG Midgets were produced. *Dave Gooley*

This early Midget brochure outlines the car's refinements, including the chrome grille and bumpers and side curtains that predated roll-up windows. *Collection of the author*

59hp at 5750rpm and gave the little car a top speed of 90 mph. More importantly, the Mark II had locking doors, wind-up glass windows, and semi-elliptic rear springs, replacing the quarter-elliptic springs used in the Mark I.

In 1966, the Mark III Midget was introduced (GAN.4), with a folding convertible top instead of the removable top of the earlier versions. The engine was a version of the 1275cc unit used in the Mini-Cooper S with a milder top end and a cheaper crankshaft, according to Wilson McComb. Still, it developed 65hp at 6000rpm. This engine stayed with the Midget until 1974 while the car itself underwent massive changes in its attempts to comply with developing and ever-changing American emission and crash laws. The first change was to Rostyle wheels and a black plastic grille with a central badge. Gone were the chrome slats of the past. In 1970, the Midget gained a crushable hood and a better heater.

In 1974 the GAN.6 picked up American-style bumpers and a one-inch increase in ride height. The weight went up 170lb, but the engine also grew. In place of the 1275cc four banger came a 1491cc unit that was originally used in the Triumph Spitfire. Power output of this engine was 65hp at 5500rpm. This was the same output as with the smaller unit but 500rpm lower. Rear wheel arches were squared off, after having been rounded in the GAN.4.

The Midget eventually died in 1979, as the MGB would the following year. In its time, the badge-engineered version of the original Austin-Healey Sprite sold almost a quarter-million vehicles in various Mark designations (224,899 to be exact). While the Midget never attracted the same kind of devo-

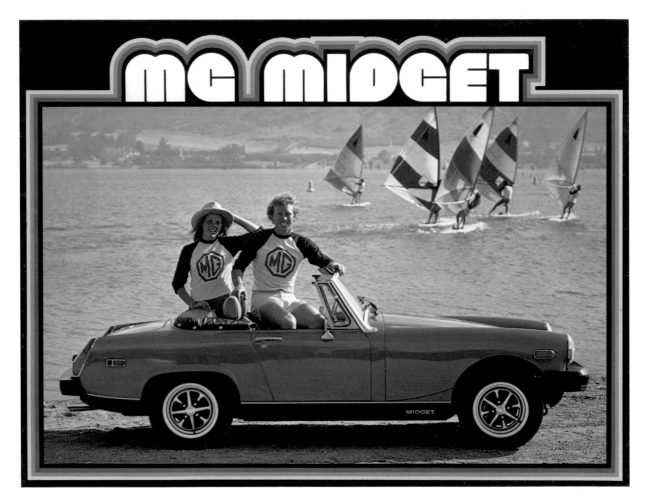

By 1979, the Midget was still "America's lowest priced sports car," but it had lost a lot of its original charm, with rubber bumpers and Rostyle wheels. *Collection of the author*

Built by British Leyland, the Midget carried its own unique identification badges.

tion that the Bugeye did, nor did it have similar competition successes, it was a best-seller and helped keep the MG name alive in an era of changing safety and emissions regulations. It might have succeeded, but British Leyland (as the corporation was now called) was "so convinced that the sun shone out of Triumph's exhaust pipe," that it produced "this bloody stupid TR7" that brought the corporation to its knees. The quotes are from John Thornley, who predicted that the TR7's styling would be out-of-date in a year. He was correct, but by that time the hemorrhaging had begun.

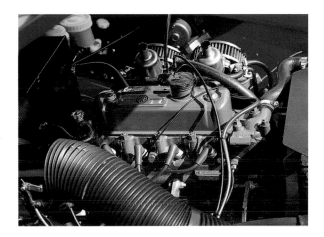

Later Midgets used a 1491cc engine that was larger than the original MGA's.

⑥

MGB/GT V8 & MGRV8

After the debacle of the MGC, the next variation for MG was a V-8-engined car built using the Rover 3500 engine of 3528cc capacity. This was the ex-Buick V-8 design that had been sold to Rover and used in the Rover 3500 sedan.

Ken Costello had made several V-8 conversions using the Rover engine, but this was the first "official" design. It was inspired by a call from MG Chief Engineer Roy Brocklehurst to British Leyland Technical Director Harry Webster. Twenty-eight days after the initial inquiry, a modified white MGB/GT was delivered to Longbridge for British Leyland Finance Director John Barber to try. He liked the car and production commenced.

Modifications to the MGB/GT to accommodate the heavier engine included stiffer front coil springs and rear leaf springs,

The British Motor Heritage Trust's MGRV8.

uprated front disc brakes, a new steering unit, wider tires, and, naturally, new badging. Top speed of the MGB/GT V8 was in the 125mph range, making the car the fastest production MG ever built.

The first V-8-powered car was completed on December 12, 1972. Nine of the first batch were left-hand-drive vehicles and were shipped to the United States for evaluation. But any hope of importing the V8 to the States was dashed by ever more stringent emission regulations and the expected small volume of cars that would have to be modified to comply.

In three years of production (1973-1976), 2,591 MGB/GT V8s were built and the program died. The reasons were manifold; the Arab oil embargo, which created a distaste for V8-engined cars; a lack of engines with which to build more cars; and the concurrent production of the rubber-bumpered four-cylinder MGB and MGB/GT, which were the mainstay of MG production at the time.

MGRV8

MG's Abingdon factory was closed in 1980. Triumph finally died in 1984 with the end of production of the Honda Ballade-based Triumph Acclaim. Austin died in 1987, leaving British Leyland with two name-plates—Rover and MG, which had continued to be used on high-performance sedans.

By 1994, the machinations of the British auto industry had created a strange world. Rover, Jaguar, and Triumph were the sole survivors of the once-mighty British Leyland Motor Holdings. The MG name was kept alive with a series of sedans, some of which were used for rallying. And as the least likely of all the marques of the com-

Above and right
If you think the MGRV8 has lines that resemble the MGB, you're right. The body shell, built by British Motor Heritage Trust, was originally designed as an MGB replacement body for restorers. It was modified and strengthened to accommodate the Rover V-8 engine as to meet collision standards.

bine to survive, Rover showing surprising strength. Americans were buying Range Rovers in sufficient numbers to earn a profit, and worldwide sales of the rugged Land Rover offered a strong operating base. True, Rover stumbled a bit with its joint operating venture with Honda (that produced the lackluster Sterling) but the company was able to recover.

Rover also held rights to the MG name, as well as that of Austin-Healey, Triumph, and a few others in the BLMH jumble. MG, though, was the genesis for a whole new line of activity.

But first, we have to look at another industry that started small but plays a important role in the MG saga.

The British Motor Industry Heritage Trust is a wellspring of information about the confused industry in Great Britain. Historians may tap the Trust's resources for information or photographs, and the people there stand ready to help.

But the Trust also became involved in the manufacturing side of the business when it began building NOS (new old stock) MGB bodies off old body bucks under the name British Motor Heritage. At first these bodies

were used in restorations, but in time they found new interests.

Enter Rover, with a nice 3.5-liter V-8 engine, which had seen a lot of service in British cars of all kinds.

As engineers are wont to do, someone at Rover decided to stuff a 3.5-liter Rover V-8 engine (the one that was derived from the old Buick mill) into one of those BMH MGB bodies. It fit. Thus was born the MGRV8. What started as an experiment soon turned into small-scale production.

Modifications were made to the BMH bodies to stiffen them and provide for such modern conveniences as wide tires and the big engine, but basically the body is unchanged from that of a later MGB. And the production run only ran for about 2,000 cars. But the MGRV8 showed that the MG name wasn't dead and could still evoke strong loyalty. The car wasn't bad, either.

Automobile Quarterly Publishing Director Jonathan Stein test drove an RV8 when it made a brief visit to the United States in the

The MGRV8's instrument panel and dash are those of a modern sports car, with a dash of old-style memories tied in. The surface is burled walnut, the instruments are white-on-black analog dials, the switches are rockers, there are decent heater controls, and the sound system is an AM/FM stereo radio with a cassette player.

summer of 1994 for an MG Car Club event in Washington, D.C.

The car was owned by Roche Bentley of the MG Owners Club of England, and he brought it to the Dulles Airport meet as an exhibit.

Stein discovered that the 3.5-liter Rover V-8 had been bored out to 3.9 liters and developed 187hp. Power reached the rear wheels through a thoroughly modern five-speed gearbox. While the MGRV8 had a modern engine, it still carried the drum rear brakes of the MGB on which it was based, as well as a leaf spring live rear axle. A limited slip differential was fitted, however.

Stein said, though, that "despite the power, beautiful interior and high build and paint quality, with its thirty-two-year-old origins and live axle, the MGRV8 does not feel like a $43,000 car. Nor can it compete with . . . a Mazda RX7, Corvette or Porsche 968."

Powering the MGRV8 is a fuel-injected 3.5-liter Rover V-8 engine, bored out to 3.9 liters and rated at 187hp. It also has all the computers and pollution control equipment of a modern engine.

The 1995 MGF. *Rover*

⑦

MGF

To paraphrase Mark Twain; "The news of MG's death has been greatly exaggerated." There *will* be another MG, and it will be built under the aegis of Rover/BMW. It will be the MGF.

The latest MG to hit the road was introduced to the public on March 7, 1995, at the Geneva Motor Show. Unfortunately, it will not be available in the United States, but the idea that MG is still alive makes lovers of the Sacred Octagon believe again.

According to Rover Cars in England, the MGF will be available in two forms—MGF 1.8i and 1.8iVVC, both powered by variations of Rover's award-winning 16-valve 1796cc four-cylinder "K" Series engine. In the 1.8i, the engine is rated at 120ps at 5500rpm. The VVC engine uses variable valve control to generate 145ps at 7000rpm.

What is most exciting is that the engine is mounted transversely behind the passenger compartment, ahead of the rear wheels, in true mid-engine form. Power gets to the rear wheels through a five-speed PG1 manual transmission.

Rover engineers said they chose the mid-engine layout after examining an assortment of other drivetrain configuration possibilities. Mid-engine/rear wheel drive was chosen "because of its inherent balance with high levels of grip and optimum handling. Under acceleration, weight transfer onto the driven rear wheels gives outstanding traction and the mid-engine layout also provides further benefits, steering being uncompromised by drive torque and high front axle weight."

Performance is on a par with or better than anything MG enthusiasts have known; 0-60mph in 8.5 seconds and a top speed of 120mph with the 1.8i; 0-60mph in 7 seconds and a top speed of 130mph with the VVC.

Variable Valve Control is a mechanism developed by Rover Group's powertrain engineers. Contained within the cylinder head, the mechanism allows the opening period of the inlet valves to be varied by altering the rotational speed of each cam lobe. The unit is hydraulically activated and controlled by the electronic engine management system.

Front and rear suspensions are by double wishbones, with tuned compliance steer characteristics and a high ratio steering rack. The MGF uses interconnected Hydragas units as the springing mechanism. Hydragas is a modern version of the hydraulic springing mechanism used in the MG1100 front-wheel-drive sedan of the early 1970s. What goes around comes around.

Cosmetically, the MGF looks uncannily like a mix of an MGB and a Mazda Miata. The front end has a curved hood line and a traditional MG badge, which has been redesigned

slightly but will still warm the cockles of MG lovers' hearts. The vertical bars of the MGA, MGB, MGC, and even the early MG Midgets are gone, however. In their place is a grille/front bumper combination that looks alarmingly like the rubber baby buggy bumper MGB. The instrument panel consists of a large speedometer and tachometer with two smaller accessory gauges. As with all modern cars there is a center console with the shifter and heater and sound system controls.

Internal storage is provided by a large glovebox, cassette holder, and cup holders in

The modern interior of the MGF shows black-on-white instruments in a padded dash, dual air bags, leather seats, and a center console that wasn't even considered for the earlier models. *Rover*

the center console. Two sets of golf clubs will be accommodated in the rear trunk, while the front compartment holds the spare tire and battery.

The body design is a result of a partnership between Rover Group and Mayflower's Motor Panels Coventry operation. The body is extremely rigid and exhibits a high level of torsional stiffness.

Built on a 93.5in wheelbase, the MGF is 154.1in long overall, 64.1in wide, and 49.8in high with the top raised. It weighs 2,332lb. A driver's airbag is standard, with the passenger's airbag optional.

Prices quoted for the MGF are around $25,600 for the 1.8i and around $30,000 for a fully equipped VVC version.

The MGF, introduced in 1995 by the Rover Group, is the latest iteration in the long line of MG sports cars. It is mid-engined and powered by a Rover V-8.

Index